Blink and it's over.

Nilu Natarajan

Presentation by *BookLeaf Publishing*

Web: www.bookleafpub.com

E-mail: info@bookleafpub.com

ISBN: 9789357745277

First edition 2023

Dedicated to my daughter, Nimo.

PREFACE

Inspired by the small things in life. Light hearted - avocation, This book takes you through beauty as seen through my eyes.

Her First Smile

As I held her in my arms, a cold winter's
morning,
I see a beautiful soul clinging on to me.
White as a pearl, pink as a delicate rose bud, a
beautiful sight,
Driven by dedication I hold my baby close to
me.

Arms and back sore in the last few days
I drag myself every single day.
Not known what the future holds,
But I look forward to a pleasant day.

As I feed her, her first morning milk
A babe of 3 months and a few days
I look at her with sleepy eyes
To my surprise,
The little baby gives me a smile.

With sleepy eyes I cannot believe what I see
A smiling baby or a day-dreaming me?
Drops of milk slide down her delicate lips,
I see my baby, thankful and happy, smiling at
me.

Toothless: I must name her, I think
I wish I could freeze that moment in time,
A feeling of happiness, joy & surprise
I cannot decide. I cannot decide. I cannot decide.

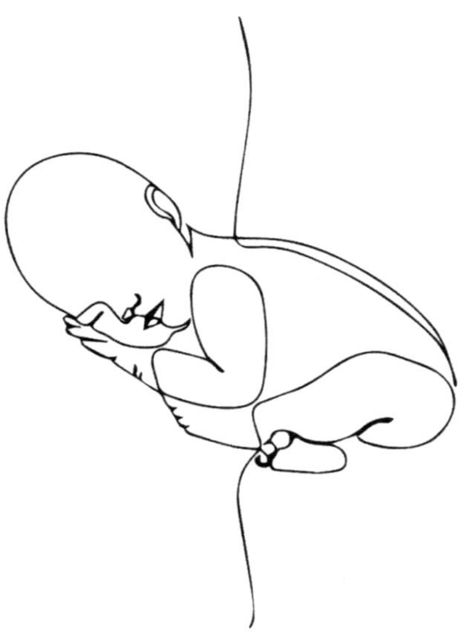

The Boat Woman

As she paddled into the horizon
She wondered if there was more to life?
Born into a family of the sea
She knew this was her destiny.

Days went by going back and forth between two
island nations
Talking to people and listening to their stories
Every journey was different, and she wondered
how her life could be?
Had she not listened to the sea.

Would she be in a city
Or be married to a bloke and be part of high tea.
As she wondered, she had reached the shore
The man in her boat looked at her with pity.
He wondered if she was happy at all doing what
she did
Or should he save her from this life.
She immediately sensed the man
And told him not to worry
She did not need his help or pity.

A proud lady of the sea, she was
She knew she had a purpose in life

The purpose of serving the sea
To serve the many men & women who used her
to flee.

Her sail was the sail to freedom,
Freedom from war & wrath.
The boatwoman was the gatekeeper for families
Sailing them to a pipe dream
To a life of freedom and liberty.

Many a tale to speak
Many a story to say
A rescuer, a gatekeeper, call her whatever you
may
Fulfilling her destiny, the boatwoman was a lady
of the sea.

Beauty

What is beauty? I ask.
The sunrise I see through my window
Or the peaceful sleep of an innocent child?
True love between people
Or a graceful tap of the feet with arms swinging
like leaves of a tree.

What is beauty? I ask.
The mystic smell of the grass, just after a drizzle
Or the beautiful stokes of a brush one tries to
capture in a moment.
The tears one cannot hold when he hears the
notes of a voice.
Or the speed of a horse as he runs with freedom
across a vast sight?

What is beauty? I ask.
Is it the Mona Lisa or the Starry Night?
Is it the face of a lady or a man?
Is it the warm breeze on my skin?
Is it the tall buildings or the jungle of man?

Beauty knows no bounds.
To each his own.
I see beauty every day in everything.
In love, in fight, in friendship & in sight.

Join in the celebration of life,
Appreciate what you have.
Beauty is in whatever you see.
Beauty is at wherever you are Be.

The Temple Flower

Bright and beautiful colours of gold
Adorn the beautiful deity of manifold
A vision of beauty & grace
I am enchanted by the sight I face.

Made by a simple man
A garland of tens and hundreds
I wonder if he knows
That he makes something that moves mountains.

A sight so beautiful by day
Comes to end by night.
The temple flowers adorned around Him & at His feet
Becomes useless and is thrown by.

Life they must still have, I believe,
I want to give them a new purpose.
A purpose of beauty and divinity,
Or a purpose to enhance the beauty of a lady.

Sow them back in the earth,
Hoping for a new birth,
The flowers that will live only for a day,
And bring beauty again to display.

Nimo

Nimo Nimo Little Star,
How I Wonder what you are?
You're full of light and funny stories
That makes me laugh till I pee.

Crazy, intelligent, caring, sweet
You're always looking for a special treat.
Maggi, pasta, all that's junk,
You wish all year you could dunk.
You need to have a balanced diet,
So that your mind can work at the speed of light.

Born out of a prayer, my sweet little baby,
I'm sure you will grow up to be a successful
lady.
SS, Literature, Maths & Language,
I know you work so hard to get knowledge.
It's a part of growing up,
Which you will appreciate soon enough.

Early to rise & early to bed,
You have made this rule hard to forget.
Changed our lives in every way,
We are glad to be this way.
Nimo Nimo Little Star,
One day I'm sure you will become a Superstar!

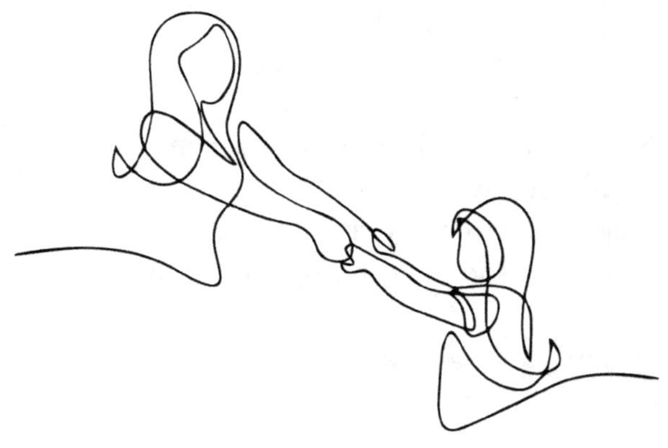

Starry Night

Oh starry night, what secrets do you hide?
You see everybody living their stories and their
plight.
A rich man who wants to become richer
A poor man who looks for hope
A mother singing to her lad
A man wondering about his horoscope.

Stars made up of hydrogen & helium
Light years away from us
Do they see us everyday, I wonder
What mysteries may they find & discover?

A story for every man
A story in every man
Jealousy, greed & pride
Some & more the stars may find.
Hopefully something dignified.

Far far away they shine bright
Gleaming at little earthlings who follow the
light.
Majestic & beautiful,
I wonder,
What other secrets may they hold?

Appa

He who shy away from the light
He who stays awake for his daughter every night
He who held her hand when she needed help
He who understands the words unsaid.

He who quietly goes about his day
Never complains, never rests, keeps it low
Let his lady be the centre
And his daughter is close though.

Many a secret he may hold,
The best one yet, his love untold.

70 years of life, 70 years of toil,
He is the man whom I run to,
When I find myself in turmoil.

I wonder how I would handle things,
If he wasn't around.
A fear grips within me,
Words that cannot be spoken about.

A warrior at heart, love in the soul,
Mom & I are thankful for the love you shower
on us, manifold.

Running

Runnin, Runnin, Runnin,
Running from myself
Running from everything I stood for.
Running from ties,
Running from heartaches,
Running from work,
Running from heartbreaks.
Running from money,
Running from responsibility,
Running from joy,
Running to destroy.
Destroy myself to be born again.
Born better.
Reborn to not be contained.
Run to joy
Run to love
Run to everything I believe,
I stand for it.

Caffeinated Sunrise

As I pour myself a hot brew,
The smell intoxicates my senses
Wide open my eyes,
I look for a peaceful and calming experience.

While everyone is asleep,
The sun yet to rise,
On a chilly morning I sit alone,
With just my coffee and i.

As I scroll through the news today,
And sip a tumbler of hot brew,
A fleeting memory crosses my mind,
When I had my first brew.

At an age of 7 or so.
Back in my grandmother's house.
I am woken by my uncle at 5am
With a tumbler of hot coffee and davara.
The smell of coffee fills the air, I smell it in my
sleep.
I know uncle has come to the bedroom ready
with our bed-coffee.

A slow smile lights my face,
Time has fleeted past, I see.
Many years have gone by,
I am now the good-morning, coffee mommy.

This moment

As I think past
Nostalgic and all
I think about my mistakes
But no regrets at all.
Learning and moving
Never stop.
Jumping through hoops of joy and sadness
And working my @$$ off.
After more than a decade,
I look at my future,
Never would have guessed this peace
A peace I am comfortable with.
Early morning wake ups, early bedtimes
Im happy with myself
Happy with this moment in time.

Shooting star

Would you be my shooting star?
And grant me my wish?
Burning up in the atmosphere
As you reach Earth
I see a ray so beautiful and
Make my eyes glow.
Beauty in the speed
Beauty in the light
Beauty in just being
In star-struck delight.
I wish a million wishes
At Least one wish come true.
Would you grant my wish, oh Shooting star
A wish I hope comes true.

Salt of the Earth

We meet a million people in our lives
You are a special one.
A kind and honest man
Deep as the rivers flow.

True to the bones
Love so strong
A believer of values
Traditions and all.
A man of great strength
A heart of a lion.
Admired by men
Do you see them?

Be careful, I say
They look at you in envy.
Have a dagger in your pocket
A smile on your face
Be prepared to give the sleight of hand to many.

All this and more to the serious man I know
A keeper of hearts
A keeper of good faith
A killer of lies
Killer of pain..

Stay strong the salt of the earth
Stay brave the salt of the earth
Stay clean the salt of the earth
Stay fearless, the salt of the earth.

The Taj

Beautiful she is in her majestic glory
White, pink or pearly she holds a mystic story
The creator in all his pride and love he plays
poetry
A poetry to live in all eternity.

Many a people see the love
Many a people see the pride
Many a people see the wonder
Many people see the plight.

Myths and stories surround the maker
Sadness and despair in the gouged eyes of the
craftsmen
Barbarous tales told by the walls of the Taj
If only you could see beyond the marbles and
gleam.

Oh what a beauty!
Oh what a wonder!
Majestic she stands
Against all plunders.

One must witness the grandness and beauty.
Walls of glory, walls of glory, walls of glory.

Beautiful forest

The scent of sweet grass
Dew drops still visible
Misty clouds
In a silent jungle.

Animals of prey walk
Far and wide,
Birds and deers
All in plain sight.

The serene beauty
The chill in the air
I suddenly feel silence in the air.

Walking ahead of me in a majestic animal
Eyes of jade and paws of thunder
Powerful and calm the striped Bagh walks
Looking at me with ease and calm.

I am reduced in size
I feel so small.
I wonder what it will take of him
To show his strength in all.

A learning of humility
A learning of calm
I now realise I am in his place
Should I be afraid?

"Be afraid. Be cautious.
Make sure you don't run and hide.
Now you know I give you space to live.
Take it and leave, or else, die."

Enchanted

As she looks into the river
A reflection of enchantment
Golden light throwing more beauty
Of gold and diamonds.

Eyes bright and wide
Eyelids long as the sea
A smile that will throw me off
Oh what a beauty!

Fingers that touch the silver river
I want to be beneath
Feel the warmth of her fingers
Enchanted beauty.

Hair like the river
Never-ending shining flow
Giving away a scent
Of jasmine and rose.

Enchanted beauty
Who are you?
Who are you?
Who are you?

Zephyr

Zephyr in the sky I feel, on her skin
Chilly mornings, birds chirping
Far away from her home.

Quicker than the sunburst, she is flying
Speeding through years
Trying to remember when it all began.

Faster, Stronger, Calmer
Wiser, smarter, better
In every way she can.

A world of opportunities
A world to lend a hand
A world to conquer.

Hello Mr. Moon

Blue moonbeams in the sky
Covering like a Turkish carpet
Beautiful rays of light
Giving us the last glimpse of light in the sky.

A day well worked
A day well earned
A day of satisfaction
A day of love and no return.

Beauty is an understatement of what I see
Magical disbelief.
As the sun sets before my eyes
I look at Mr. Moon and say, Hi!

Hello! How are you?
Nothing much has changed since yesterday.
Precious, beautiful, I treasure my life,
I am glad to see you again.

So many faces you have,
Which one is your best?
I wish I could be you,
Change myself everyday
A new me every night
What do you say?

Haha.. You fool.
I see you.
Arent you the same one
Who had this conversation yesterday.
Pretence, deceit, drama and more,
mankind is not so different
He has a face every day to mourn.

Do your duty, stay humble,
Cut the weeds and look to grow.
Look past the mess!
Stay true and bow.

Pink

Shades of life & love
Shades of beauty & peace
Strokes of fun & laughter
Many a pink I see.

Pink in the sky
Pink in my garden
Pink in life
Pink to run away from boredom.

A colour so fascinating
White & red in it
A tinge on the cheek & lip
Or the soft hands of a baby's tip.

Beautiful and precious pink
Light up the air every year
Bringing joy and brightness
Everywhere it is near.